not The End.
A Child's Journey Through Grief

Keep turning the pages of your story.
Mari Dombkowski

By Mari Dombkowski
Illustrated By Nazar Horokhivskyi

Dedicated to Thea, Anna, Meagan, Hailey, and Kelsey - and all the other boys and girls who have lost a mom or dad.

Copyright © 2015 by Mari Dombkowski
Contact: nottheend.book@gmail.com

All rights reserved. No part of this publication may be reproduced, stored in a retrieval system or transmitted, in any form, or by any means, electronic, mechanical, recorded, photocopied, or otherwise, without the prior permission of the copyright owner, except by a reviewer who may quote brief passages in a review.

Published by: Terwilliger Publishing

Printed in China

ISBN 978-0-9965367-0-7

A Note About This Book

This book was written to give hope to children who have experienced the death of a parent. My intention is that loved ones and those working with grieving children will use these pages as a springboard for discussion and a tool for healing.

Through this true story, children can see that it is possible to continue to grow, thrive and enjoy life even after the devastating loss of a parent. The hurt they feel at the beginning of grief - that hole in their hearts - will lessen over time as they move forward with their lives.

--M.D.

If you're like me, you already know that some stories end too soon. But sometimes what you thought was the end turns out to be, well, kind of a "page-turner."

That's what happened to our family's story.

We were an average family. There was my dad, mom, little sister Anna, our dogs Bernie and Noble, and our cat Christopher

-- and me, Thea. Our family loved doing things together.

Then, one day my dad got really sick.
He had to go to the hospital in an ambulance.

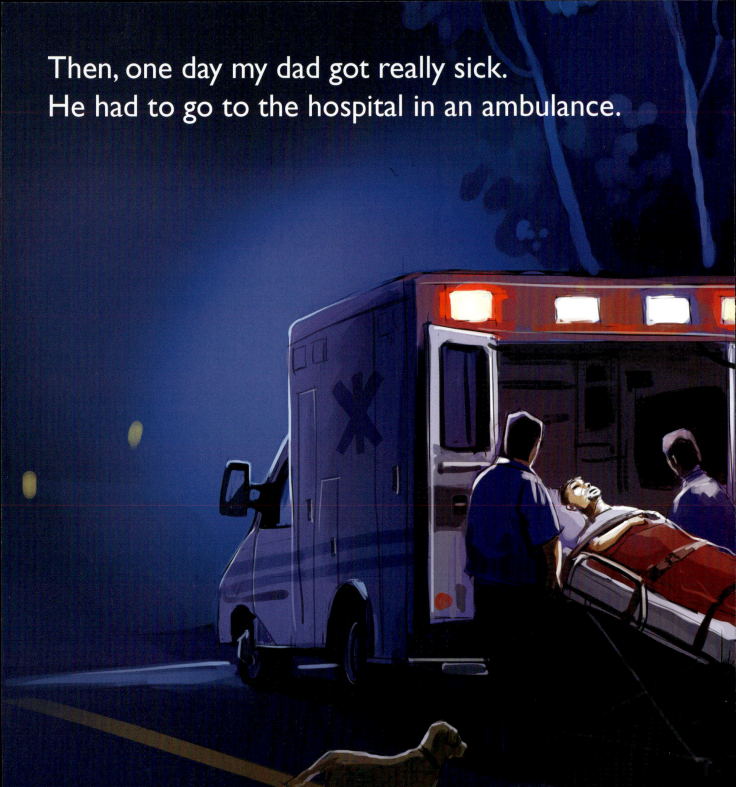

Maybe Daddy was pretending.

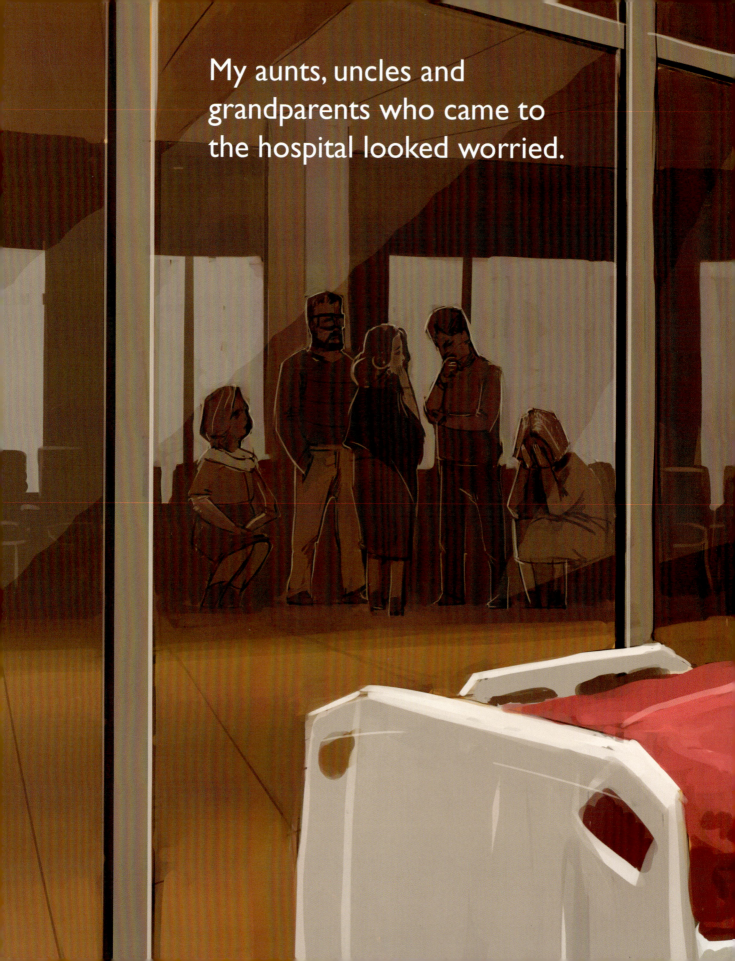

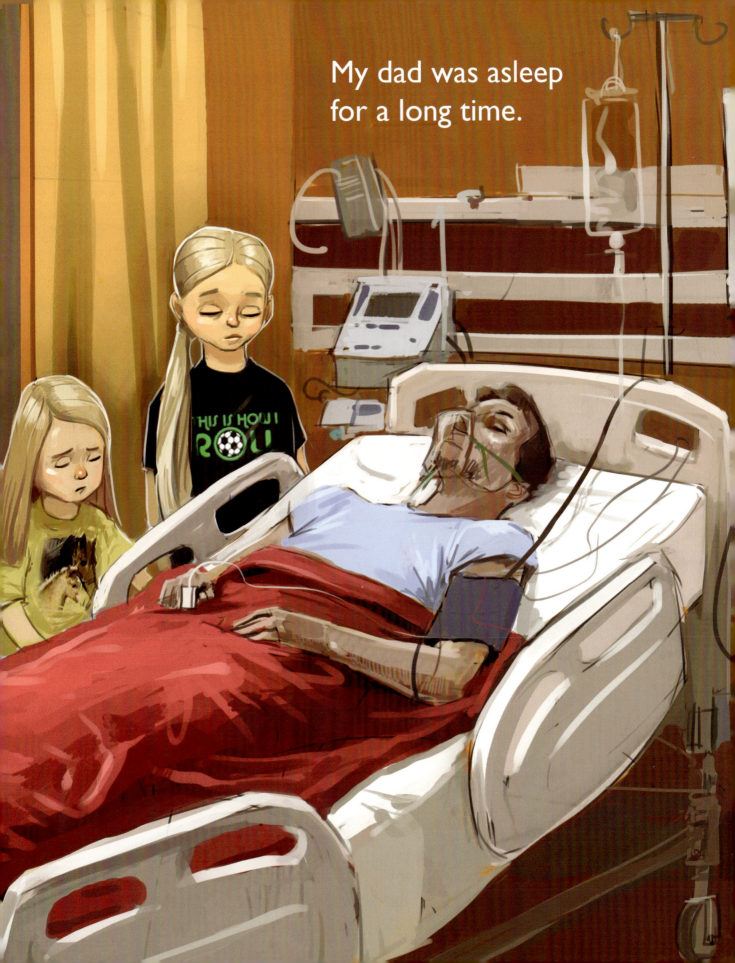

After the funeral and all the people went home, our house was lonely and sad.

My mom cried ALL the time.

Anna and I stayed in our rooms.
We did not want to talk about what had happened.

My mom turned the page every time she got out of bed to go to work.

And believe me, there were days she was really late because that page was so heavy.

Sometimes, Bernie and Noble actually turned the page for her.

My sister and I turned the page every time we went to school.

But after a little time, it became easier.

I turned the pages when I went to my soccer games or to my friends' houses for sleepovers.

Mom took a writing class and started jogging.

My sister got a new kitten and began horse-riding lessons.

As I continued my story into high school, I ran on the cross-country team and made some great friends.

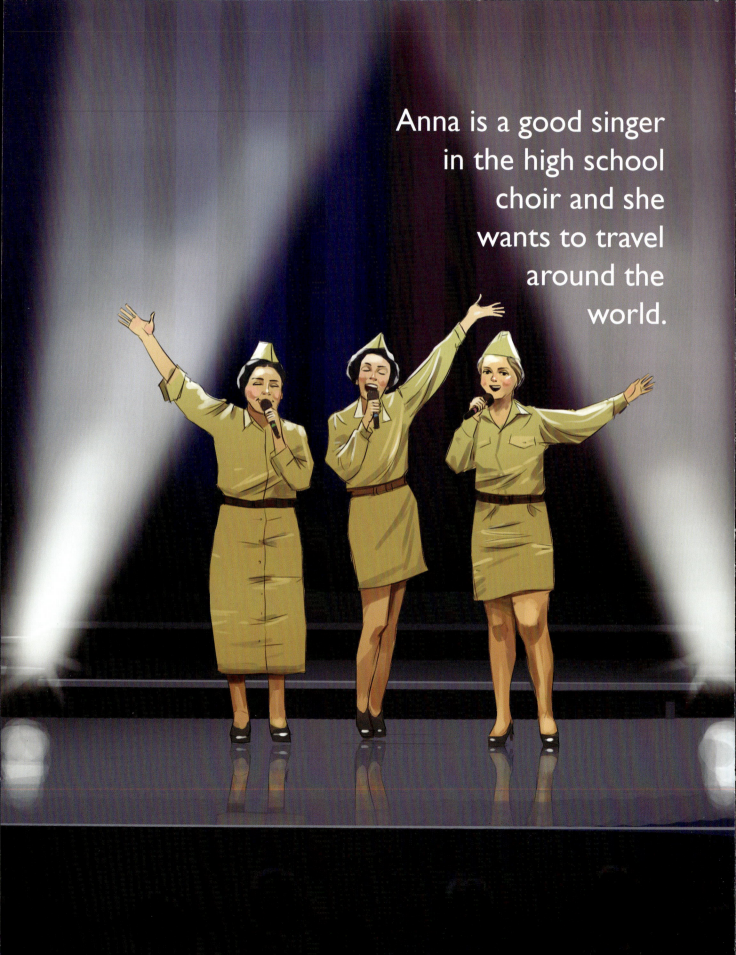

We all still have a hole in our hearts, but I think as long as we keep turning the pages of our story, the hurt will get smaller and smaller.

Our story is not over – and neither is yours.

Based on the true story of Mari and her two daughers, Anna & Thea (2015).

nottheend.book@gmail.com